Badass Bitches are Born in September

> *"keep taking chances - make life your bitch, have beautiful experiences and never give up"*

Date: /   /

_____

_____

_____

_____

_____

_____

_____

_____

_____

_____

_____

_____

_____

_____

_____

_____

_____

_____

_____

_____

THINGS TO BE GRATEFUL FOR TODAY

"Have dreams and dream big! Dream without fear"

Date: /   /

_____

_____

_____

_____

_____

_____

_____

_____

_____

_____

_____

_____

_____

_____

_____

_____

_____

_____

_____

_____

_____

THINGS TO BE GRATEFUL FOR TODAY

"Believe in miracles but above all believe in yourself!"

Date: /   /

_____

_____

_____

_____

_____

_____

_____

_____

_____

_____

_____

_____

_____

_____

_____

_____

_____

_____

_____

THINGS TO BE GRATEFUL FOR TODAY

"Let your dreams be as big as your desire to succeed"

Date: /   /

_____
_____
_____
_____
_____
_____
_____
_____
_____
_____
_____
_____
_____
_____
_____
_____
_____
_____
_____
_____

THINGS TO BE GRATEFUL FOR TODAY

> *"Never downgrade your dreams, reach for the stars and believe in your self power"*

Date: / /

_____
_____
_____
_____
_____
_____
_____
_____
_____
_____
_____
_____
_____
_____
_____
_____
_____
_____
_____
_____
_____

THINGS TO BE GRATEFUL FOR TODAY

> *"They say I dream too big. I say they think too small"* - Unknown

Date: /   /

_____

_____

_____

_____

_____

_____

_____

_____

_____

_____

_____

_____

_____

_____

_____

_____

_____

THINGS TO BE GRATEFUL FOR TODAY

Date: /   /

_____

_____

_____

_____

_____

_____

_____

_____

_____

_____

_____

_____

_____

_____

_____

_____

_____

_____

THINGS TO BE GRATEFUL FOR TODAY

"Your driving force and your power lies within you and the size of your dreams, never give up!"

Date: /   /

_____
_____
_____
_____
_____
_____
_____
_____
_____
_____
_____
_____
_____
_____
_____
_____
_____
_____
_____
_____
_____

THINGS TO BE GRATEFUL FOR TODAY

Date: /   /

THINGS TO BE GRATEFUL FOR TODAY

Date: /   /

_____
_____
_____
_____
_____
_____
_____
_____
_____
_____
_____
_____
_____
_____
_____
_____
_____
_____
_____
_____
_____
_____

THINGS TO BE GRATEFUL FOR TODAY

> *"Your dreams and your goals are the seeds of your own success"*

Date: /   /

_____

_____

_____

_____

_____

_____

_____

_____

_____

_____

_____

_____

_____

_____

_____

_____

_____

_____

_____

THINGS TO BE GRATEFUL FOR TODAY

"Never give up, keep going no matter what!"

Date: /   /

_____
_____
_____
_____
_____
_____
_____
_____
_____
_____
_____
_____
_____
_____
_____
_____
_____
_____
_____
_____
_____

THINGS TO BE GRATEFUL FOR TODAY

Date: /   /

_____

_____

_____

_____

_____

_____

_____

_____

_____

_____

_____

_____

_____

_____

_____

_____

_____

_____

THINGS TO BE GRATEFUL FOR TODAY

> *"If you never give up you become unbeatable, just keep going!"*

Date: /   /

THINGS TO BE GRATEFUL FOR TODAY

Date: /   /

THINGS TO BE GRATEFUL FOR TODAY

> *"Change your life today. Don't gamble on the future, act now, without delay."* — *Simone de Beauvoir*

Date: / /

_____

_____
_____
_____
_____
_____
_____
_____
_____
_____
_____
_____
_____
_____
_____
_____
_____
_____
_____

THINGS TO BE GRATEFUL FOR TODAY

Date: /   /

_____

_____

_____

_____

_____

_____

_____

_____

_____

_____

_____

_____

_____

_____

_____

_____

_____

_____

_____

_____

_____

THINGS TO BE GRATEFUL FOR TODAY

"Aim for the stars to keep your dreams alive"

Date: /   /

_____

_____

_____

_____

_____

_____

_____

_____

_____

_____

_____

_____

_____

_____

_____

_____

_____

_____

_____

THINGS TO BE GRATEFUL FOR TODAY

"When life gives you lemons, add a little gin and tonic"

Date: /   /
_____

_____
_____
_____
_____
_____
_____
_____
_____
_____
_____
_____
_____
_____
_____
_____
_____
_____
_____
_____

THINGS TO BE GRATEFUL FOR TODAY

> *"There are no limits to what you can achieve if you believe in your dreams"*

Date: /   /

THINGS TO BE GRATEFUL FOR TODAY

"When you feel you are defeated, just remember, you have the power to move on, it is all in your mind"

Date: /   /

_____
_____
_____
_____
_____
_____
_____
_____
_____
_____
_____
_____
_____
_____
_____
_____
_____
_____

THINGS TO BE GRATEFUL FOR TODAY

"Don't just dream your dreams, make them happen!"

Date: /   /

_____

_____

_____

_____

_____

_____

_____

_____

_____

_____

_____

_____

_____

_____

_____

_____

_____

_____

_____

_____

_____

THINGS TO BE GRATEFUL FOR TODAY

Date: /   /

THINGS TO BE GRATEFUL FOR TODAY

"You are the creator of your own opportunities"

Date: /   /

_____

_____

_____

_____

_____

_____

_____

_____

_____

_____

_____

_____

_____

_____

_____

_____

_____

_____

_____

_____

THINGS TO BE GRATEFUL FOR TODAY

Date: /   /

_____

_____

_____

_____

_____

_____

_____

_____

_____

_____

_____

_____

_____

_____

_____

_____

_____

_____

_____

_____

THINGS TO BE GRATEFUL FOR TODAY

"Success is not a place or a destination, it is a way of thinking while always having a new goal in mind"

Date: /   /

THINGS TO BE GRATEFUL FOR TODAY

Date: / /

_____

_____

_____

_____

_____

_____

_____

_____

_____

_____

_____

_____

_____

_____

_____

_____

_____

_____

_____

_____

THINGS TO BE GRATEFUL FOR TODAY

Date: /   /

_____

_____
_____
_____
_____
_____
_____
_____
_____
_____
_____
_____
_____
_____
_____
_____
_____
_____
_____
_____

THINGS TO BE GRATEFUL FOR TODAY

> *"Never loose confidence in your dreams, there will be obstacles and defeats, but you will always win if you persist"*

Date: /   /

THINGS TO BE GRATEFUL FOR TODAY

> *""Never wait for someone else to validate your existence, you are the creator of your own destiny"*

Date: /   /

_____

_____

_____

_____

_____

_____

_____

_____

_____

_____

_____

_____

_____

_____

_____

_____

_____

_____

THINGS TO BE GRATEFUL FOR TODAY

"Dreams are the energy that power your life"

Date: /   /
_____

_____
_____
_____
_____
_____
_____
_____
_____
_____
_____
_____
_____
_____
_____
_____
_____
_____
_____
_____

THINGS TO BE GRATEFUL FOR TODAY

"Dreams make things happen, nothing is impossible as long as you believe." - Anonymous

Date: /   /

THINGS TO BE GRATEFUL FOR TODAY

Date: /   /

_____

_____

_____

_____

_____

_____

_____

_____

_____

_____

_____

_____

_____

_____

_____

_____

_____

_____

_____

_____

_____

THINGS TO BE GRATEFUL FOR TODAY

Date: /   /

THINGS TO BE GRATEFUL FOR TODAY

"Everything you dream is possible as long as you believe in yourself"

Date: /   /

_____

_____

_____

_____

_____

_____

_____

_____

_____

_____

_____

_____

_____

_____

_____

_____

_____

THINGS TO BE GRATEFUL FOR TODAY

"Dream big, it's the first step to success" - Anonymous

Date: /   /

_____
_____
_____
_____
_____
_____
_____
_____
_____
_____
_____
_____
_____
_____
_____
_____
_____
_____
_____
_____

THINGS TO BE GRATEFUL FOR TODAY

> *"A successful person is someone that understands temporary defeat as a learning process, never give up!"*

Date: /   /
_____

_____
_____
_____
_____
_____
_____
_____
_____
_____
_____
_____
_____
_____
_____
_____
_____
_____
_____
_____
_____

THINGS TO BE GRATEFUL FOR TODAY

"Motivation comes from working on our dreams and from taking action to achieve our goals"

Date: /   /

_____

_____

_____

_____

_____

_____

_____

_____

_____

_____

_____

_____

_____

_____

_____

_____

_____

_____

THINGS TO BE GRATEFUL FOR TODAY

Date: /   /

_____

_____

_____

_____

_____

_____

_____

_____

_____

_____

_____

_____

_____

_____

_____

_____

_____

_____

_____

THINGS TO BE GRATEFUL FOR TODAY

> *"Your mission in life should be to thrive and not merely survive"*

Date: /   /

THINGS TO BE GRATEFUL FOR TODAY

"Doing what you believe in, and going after your dreams will only result in success." - Anonymous

Date: /   /

THINGS TO BE GRATEFUL FOR TODAY

"The right time to start something new is now"

Date: /   /

_____

_____

_____

_____

_____

_____

_____

_____

_____

_____

_____

_____

_____

_____

_____

_____

_____

_____

THINGS TO BE GRATEFUL FOR TODAY

"Be brave, fight for what you believe in and make your dreams a reality." - Anonymous

Date: / /

_____

_____

_____

_____

_____

_____

_____

_____

_____

_____

_____

_____

_____

_____

_____

_____

_____

_____

_____

THINGS TO BE GRATEFUL FOR TODAY

> *"Put more energy into your dreams than
> Into your fears and you will see positive results"*

Date: /   /

_____

_____
_____
_____
_____
_____
_____
_____
_____
_____
_____
_____
_____
_____
_____
_____
_____
_____
_____
_____

THINGS TO BE GRATEFUL FOR TODAY

"Let your dreams be bigger than your fears and your actions louder than your words." - Anonymous

Date: /   /

_____

_____
_____
_____
_____
_____
_____
_____
_____
_____
_____
_____
_____
_____
_____
_____
_____
_____
_____
_____
_____

THINGS TO BE GRATEFUL FOR TODAY

Date: /   /

THINGS TO BE GRATEFUL FOR TODAY

Date: /   /
_____

_____
_____
_____
_____
_____
_____
_____
_____
_____
_____
_____
_____
_____
_____
_____
_____
_____
_____

THINGS TO BE GRATEFUL FOR TODAY

"Dream. Believe. Create. Succeed" - Anonymous

Date: /   /

_____
_____
_____
_____
_____
_____
_____
_____
_____
_____
_____
_____
_____
_____
_____
_____
_____
_____
_____
_____

THINGS TO BE GRATEFUL FOR TODAY

Date: /   /

_____

_____

_____

_____

_____

_____

_____

_____

_____

_____

_____

_____

_____

_____

_____

_____

_____

_____

_____

_____

THINGS TO BE GRATEFUL FOR TODAY

Date: /   /

_____

_____

_____

_____

_____

_____

_____

_____

_____

_____

_____

_____

_____

_____

_____

_____

_____

_____

_____

THINGS TO BE GRATEFUL FOR TODAY

"Difficulties are nothing more than opportunities in disguise, keep on trying and you will succeed"

Date: /   /

THINGS TO BE GRATEFUL FOR TODAY

> *"To achieve our dreams we must first overcome our fear of failure"*

Date: /   /

THINGS TO BE GRATEFUL FOR TODAY

Date: /   /
_____

_____
_____
_____
_____
_____
_____
_____
_____
_____
_____
_____
_____
_____
_____
_____
_____
_____
_____

THINGS TO BE GRATEFUL FOR TODAY

"Use failure as a motivation tool not as a sign of defeat"

Date: /   /

_____

_____

_____

_____

_____

_____

_____

_____

_____

_____

_____

_____

_____

_____

_____

_____

_____

_____

_____

THINGS TO BE GRATEFUL FOR TODAY

*"Never let your dreams die for fear of failure,
defeat is just temporary; your dreams are your power"*

Date: /   /

THINGS TO BE GRATEFUL FOR TODAY

"A failure is a lesson, not a loss. It is a temporary and sometimes necessary detour, not a dead end"

Date: /   /

_____
_____
_____
_____
_____
_____
_____
_____
_____
_____
_____
_____
_____
_____
_____
_____
_____
_____
_____
_____

THINGS TO BE GRATEFUL FOR TODAY

"Have faith in the future but above all in yourself"

Date: /   /

_____

_____
_____
_____
_____
_____
_____
_____
_____
_____
_____
_____
_____
_____
_____
_____
_____
_____
_____
_____
_____
_____

THINGS TO BE GRATEFUL FOR TODAY

"Those who live in the past limit their future"
- Anonymous

Date: /   /

_____

_____
_____
_____
_____
_____
_____
_____
_____
_____
_____
_____
_____
_____
_____
_____
_____
_____
_____
_____

THINGS TO BE GRATEFUL FOR TODAY

Date: /   /

THINGS TO BE GRATEFUL FOR TODAY

"Never let your doubt blind your goals, for your future lies in your ability, not your failure" — Anonymous

Date: /   /

_____
_____
_____
_____
_____
_____
_____
_____
_____
_____
_____
_____
_____
_____
_____
_____
_____
_____
_____
_____
_____

THINGS TO BE GRATEFUL FOR TODAY

Date: /   /

_____

_____

_____

_____

_____

_____

_____

_____

_____

_____

_____

_____

_____

_____

_____

_____

_____

_____

THINGS TO BE GRATEFUL FOR TODAY

"Laughter is the shock absorber that softens and minimizes the bumps of life" — Anonymous

Date: /   /

_____

_____

_____

_____

_____

_____

_____

_____

_____

_____

_____

_____

_____

_____

_____

_____

_____

_____

_____

THINGS TO BE GRATEFUL FOR TODAY

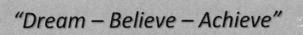

"Dream – Believe – Achieve"

Date: / /

_____

_____
_____
_____
_____
_____
_____
_____
_____
_____
_____
_____
_____
_____
_____
_____
_____
_____
_____

THINGS TO BE GRATEFUL FOR TODAY

> *"Make your own destiny. Don't wait for it to come to you, life is not a rehearsal"* — Anonymous

Date: /   /

THINGS TO BE GRATEFUL FOR TODAY

"If you want to feel rich, just count all the things you have that money can't buy" — *Anonymous*

Date: /   /
_____

_____
_____
_____
_____
_____
_____
_____
_____
_____
_____
_____
_____
_____
_____
_____
_____
_____
_____

THINGS TO BE GRATEFUL FOR TODAY

"Never give up on a dream just because of the time it will take to accomplish it. The time will pass anyway." – Anonymous

Date: /   /
_____

_____
_____
_____
_____
_____
_____
_____
_____
_____
_____
_____
_____
_____
_____
_____
_____
_____
_____
_____
_____

THINGS TO BE GRATEFUL FOR TODAY

"I am never a failure until I begin blaming others"
- Anonymous

Date: /   /

THINGS TO BE GRATEFUL FOR TODAY

"Your only limitation is your imagination" — *Anonymous*

Date: /   /

_____

_____

_____

_____

_____

_____

_____

_____

_____

_____

_____

_____

_____

_____

_____

_____

_____

_____

_____

THINGS TO BE GRATEFUL FOR TODAY

Date: /   /

_____

_____

_____

_____

_____

_____

_____

_____

_____

_____

_____

_____

_____

_____

_____

_____

_____

_____

_____

_____

THINGS TO BE GRATEFUL FOR TODAY

Date: /   /

THINGS TO BE GRATEFUL FOR TODAY

Date: /   /

_____

_____

_____

_____

_____

_____

_____

_____

_____

_____

_____

_____

_____

_____

_____

_____

_____

_____

_____

_____

_____

THINGS TO BE GRATEFUL FOR TODAY

"Never let defeat have the last word" — Anonymous

Date: /   /

_____

_____

_____

_____

_____

_____

_____

_____

_____

_____

_____

_____

_____

_____

_____

_____

_____

_____

THINGS TO BE GRATEFUL FOR TODAY

Date: /   /

_____

_____

_____

_____

_____

_____

_____

_____

_____

_____

_____

_____

_____

_____

_____

_____

_____

_____

_____

_____

THINGS TO BE GRATEFUL FOR TODAY

Date: /   /

THINGS TO BE GRATEFUL FOR TODAY

Date: /   /
_____

_____
_____
_____
_____
_____
_____
_____
_____
_____
_____
_____
_____
_____
_____
_____
_____
_____
_____
_____

THINGS TO BE GRATEFUL FOR TODAY

Date: /   /

THINGS TO BE GRATEFUL FOR TODAY

"Dreams don't come true. Dreams are true"
— Anonymous

Date: /   /

_____

_____

_____

_____

_____

_____

_____

_____

_____

_____

_____

_____

_____

_____

_____

_____

_____

_____

_____

_____

THINGS TO BE GRATEFUL FOR TODAY

Date: /   /

_____

THINGS TO BE GRATEFUL FOR TODAY

> *"A journey of a thousand miles must begin with a single step."* – Lao Tzu

Date: / /

THINGS TO BE GRATEFUL FOR TODAY

Date: /   /

THINGS TO BE GRATEFUL FOR TODAY

"You risk more when you don't take any risks"

Date: /   /

THINGS TO BE GRATEFUL FOR TODAY

> *"A diamond is a chunk of coal that made good under pressure"* — *Anonymous*

Date: /   /

_____

_____
_____
_____
_____
_____
_____
_____
_____
_____
_____
_____
_____
_____
_____
_____
_____
_____
_____
_____

THINGS TO BE GRATEFUL FOR TODAY

Date: /   /

_____

_____

_____

_____

_____

_____

_____

_____

_____

_____

_____

_____

_____

_____

_____

_____

_____

_____

THINGS TO BE GRATEFUL FOR TODAY

"All our tomorrows depend on today" — *Anonymous*

Date: /   /

_____

THINGS TO BE GRATEFUL FOR TODAY

Date: /   /

_____

_____

_____

_____

_____

_____

_____

_____

_____

_____

_____

_____

_____

_____

_____

_____

_____

_____

_____

THINGS TO BE GRATEFUL FOR TODAY

"Dream is not what you see in sleep, dream is the thing which does not let you sleep" — *Anonymous*

Date: /   /

THINGS TO BE GRATEFUL FOR TODAY

Date: /   /

THINGS TO BE GRATEFUL FOR TODAY

> *"Dreams give purpose to your life and meaning to your existence"*

Date: /   /

_____
_____
_____
_____
_____
_____
_____
_____
_____
_____
_____
_____
_____
_____
_____
_____
_____
_____
_____
_____
_____

THINGS TO BE GRATEFUL FOR TODAY

Date: /   /

THINGS TO BE GRATEFUL FOR TODAY

"Follow your heart and your dreams will come true"
– Anonymous

Date: /   /
_____

_____

_____

_____

_____

_____

_____

_____

_____

_____

_____

_____

_____

_____

_____

_____

_____

_____

_____

_____

_____

THINGS TO BE GRATEFUL FOR TODAY

Date: /   /

THINGS TO BE GRATEFUL FOR TODAY

Date: /   /

THINGS TO BE GRATEFUL FOR TODAY

"Difficult roads often lead to beautiful destinations"

Date: /   /
_____

_____
_____
_____
_____
_____
_____
_____
_____
_____
_____
_____
_____
_____
_____
_____
_____
_____
_____
_____
_____
_____

THINGS TO BE GRATEFUL FOR TODAY

"The road to success is always full of surprises and temporary failures, real success comes to those who persist"

Date: /   /

THINGS TO BE GRATEFUL FOR TODAY

Date: /   /

___

THINGS TO BE GRATEFUL FOR TODAY

Date: /   /

THINGS TO BE GRATEFUL FOR TODAY

"To live a creative life, we must lose our fear of being wrong" - Anonymous

Date: /   /

THINGS TO BE GRATEFUL FOR TODAY

Date: /   /

THINGS TO BE GRATEFUL FOR TODAY

Date: /   /

_____

_____

_____

_____

_____

_____

_____

_____

_____

_____

_____

_____

_____

_____

_____

_____

_____

THINGS TO BE GRATEFUL FOR TODAY

> *"It's not what you look at that matters,*
> *it's what you see" - Anonymous*

Date: /   /

_____

_____

_____

_____

_____

_____

_____

_____

_____

_____

_____

_____

_____

_____

_____

_____

_____

_____

THINGS TO BE GRATEFUL FOR TODAY

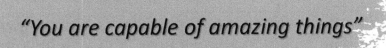

"You are capable of amazing things"

Date: /   /

_____

THINGS TO BE GRATEFUL FOR TODAY

"Believe in yourself and you will be unstoppable"

Date: /   /

_____
_____
_____
_____
_____
_____
_____
_____
_____
_____
_____
_____
_____
_____
_____
_____
_____
_____
_____
_____

THINGS TO BE GRATEFUL FOR TODAY

Date: /   /

_____

_____

_____

_____

_____

_____

_____

_____

_____

_____

_____

_____

_____

_____

_____

_____

_____

_____

_____

THINGS TO BE GRATEFUL FOR TODAY

Date: /   /

THINGS TO BE GRATEFUL FOR TODAY

"Nothing worth having comes easy" - Anonymous

Date: /   /

_____

_____

_____

_____

_____

_____

_____

_____

_____

_____

_____

_____

_____

_____

_____

_____

_____

_____

THINGS TO BE GRATEFUL FOR TODAY

"Don't Let Anyone Dull Your Sparkle"

Date: /   /

_____

_____

_____

_____

_____

_____

_____

_____

_____

_____

_____

_____

_____

_____

_____

_____

_____

_____

_____

_____

_____

_____

THINGS TO BE GRATEFUL FOR TODAY

"You can have results or excuses. Not both" – Unknown

Date: /   /

_____

_____

_____

_____

_____

_____

_____

_____

_____

_____

_____

_____

_____

_____

_____

_____

_____

_____

THINGS TO BE GRATEFUL FOR TODAY

CREATIVE JOURNALS
FACTORY

We hope you enjoyed your journal — notebook — diary. Please let us know if you liked it by writing a review, it means a lot to us.

Thank you!

Designed by: Creative Funny Journals for:

CREATIVE JOURNALS FACTORY

Made in the USA
Las Vegas, NV
22 August 2021